by Nikolai Katkov
illustrated by Steve Cox

HOUGHTON MIFFLIN HARCOURT
School Publishers

Printed in China

ISBN-13: 978-0-547-02845-3
ISBN-10: 0-547-02845-8

2 3 4 5 6 7 8 0940 18 17 16 15 14 13 12 11 10

Polly goes to the pet store.
She does not get a brown dog
or a green bird.
Polly gets a big white
polar bear.
His name is Big Pete.
He is not like most pets!

Big Pete causes big trouble, but
he does not mean to.
Big Pete races to the door when
the mail comes.
He just wants to say hello.
Polly tries to get there first...
but Big Pete is too fast.

Big Pete wants to try on
Polly's skates.
The skates are too small, and
Big Pete falls down.
Polly gives him an old scooter
to ride.
It is a better size for Pete.

The days grow hot.
Big Pete misses the frost
and snow.
Polly fills the pool with ice and
water, and Big Pete goes for a
cold swim.

Big Pete sees Polly painting a
picture, and he wants to paint a
picture too.
He uses Polly's brush.
Look at the mess he makes!

Big Pete spills paint on the floor
and walls.
He splashes paint
on the window too.
Polly wipes the walls, and Mother
mops the floor.
Big Pete washes the window.

Mother makes dinner for Polly.
Big Pete wants to eat, too.
Mother gives him lots of fish,
but Big Pete still wants more.
Big Pete is always hungry!

Mother reads a story to Polly.
Big Pete listens, too.
Listening to the story makes
him sleepy.

Polly goes to sleep, and Big Pete
goes to sleep, too.
Polly is not afraid of the dark
when Pete is there.
She has happy dreams.
Big Pete dreams, too.
His dream is about his fun day.

Responding

 Cause and Effect

What happens when Big Pete comes to Polly's house? Why does it happen? Make a chart.

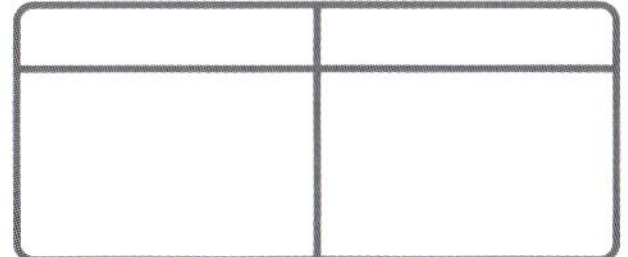

Talk About It

Text to Text Think about other books with animals that act like people. What do the animals do?

door	try
more	use
mother	want
old	wash

✔ **TARGET SKILL** **Cause and Effect**

Tell what happens and why.

✔ **TARGET STRATEGY** **Infer/Predict**

Use clues to figure out more about story parts.

GENRE A **fantasy** is a story that could not happen in real life.